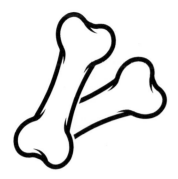

This book belongs to:

❀━❀━❀━❀━❀ ❀━❀━❀━❀

For my Dad x

First UK edition 2023

ISBN: 9798852984081

The Adventures of Ralph & Reggie
REGGIE'S BIG SPLASH

By
Karen Faulkner

ONCE UPON A TIME
IN A QUIET SUNNY TOWN,
LIVED RALPH AND REGGIE
THE HAPPIEST SHIH TZU'S AROUND.
THEY LOVED TO PLAY AND EXPLORE
IN SUNSHINE OR RAIN,
BUT REGGIE HAD A SECRET,
A FEAR HE COULDN'T EXPLAIN.

HE WAS SCARED OF WATER,

IT FILLED HIM WITH DREAD!

THE SIGHT OF A BATH MADE HIM RUN

AND HIDE ON HIS BED!

HIS HEART WOULD RACE,

HIS PAWS WOULD QUIVER,

EVEN THE SOUND OF WATER

MADE HIM SHIVER!

HE NEVER LIKED TO SWIM,
NOT EVEN A BATH.
HE'D HIDE UNDER THE TABLE
WITH HIS SQUEAKY GIRAFFE.

ONE BRIGHT SUNNY DAY,

RALPH AND REGGIE WENT TO THE PARK.

THEY MET THEIR FRIEND LUNA,

SAYING HI! WITH A BARK.

LUNA LOVED THE POND,

SHE WOULD SWIM AND TWIRL.

SPLASHING IN THE WATER

MADE LUNA A HAPPY GIRL!

RALPH TURNED TO REGGIE,
HIS GAZE SOFT AND KIND,
'ARE YOU READY TO GIVE IT A TRY
AND LEAVE YOUR FEAR BEHIND?'
REGGIE LOOKED ON
AT THE WATER SO BLUE,
HIS HEART WAS POUNDING,
BUT IT'S SOMETHING HE KNEW HE HAD TO DO.

WITH A HELPFUL LITTLE NUDGE,
RALPH LED REGGIE IN.
THE WATER WAS COOL,
IT TICKLED HIS CHIN!
STEP BY STEP REGGIE BEGAN TO SEE,
THE WATER WASN'T AS SCARY
AS HE THOUGHT IT WOULD BE!

WITH RALPH BY HIS SIDE

AND LUNA SPLASHING AHEAD,

REGGIE FOUND COURAGE

AND NO LONGER FELT DREAD.

HE PADDLED AND SPLASHED

WITH A SMILE ON HIS FACE,

KNOWING THAT THE WATER CAN BE A

VERY HAPPY PLACE!

AS THE DAY CAME TO AN END,

REGGIE HAD FACED HIS FEAR.

HE'D LEARNED TO SWIM,

AND IT BECAME CLEAR.

WITH A DASH OF COURAGE

AND FRIENDS SO KIND,

THERE'S NO FEAR THAT WE CAN'T LEAVE BEHIND.

SO ALWAYS REMEMBER
AS YOU GROW AND LEARN,
FEARS ARE JUST CHALLENGES,
WAITING FOR THEIR TURN.
LIKE REGGIE LEARNED WITH RALPH
AND LUNA CLOSE BY,
FACING YOUR FEARS
IS EASY WHEN YOU TRY!

LUNA

RALPH & REGGIE

Printed in Great Britain
by Amazon